Acknowledgements

Thanks are due to the editors of these magazines, anthologies and publishers: Staple 100 Best Poems, Interpreter's House, Quaker Monthly, Poetry Monthly, Envoi, Iron Erotica, Smiths Knoll, BBC, Stainer and Bell.

Poems have also featured in Mirehouse Poetry Competition; Lancaster Litfest Competition; Poetry on the Lake International Competition, Italy; FRED Art Alert, Cumbria; OU Sonnet Competition; Mslexia Poetry Competition; Strokestown Poetry Competition, Ireland.

Thanks also to Arts Council England for a grant to read in Italy, 2007, and to the Yorkshire Dales Millennium Trust for inclusion in the 'Hay Time' anthology.

Special thanks to Gerard Benson, Neil Curry and Myra Schneider.

Other Publications by Maggie Norton

Brantub The Dancing Bear, Random House

Poems for children in Macmillan's anthology for schools, *Read Me at School* and Scholastic's *Drama and Short Plays* and poems and stories in B.B.C. Playdays magazine.

Come Ride and *Ride Again*, poetry collections for primary schools.

Pamphlets: *Planning the Route* and *Love and Stuff.*

CONTENTS

Onions
and Other Intentions

Art Exhibition From A Narrowboat

Welcome to the Interactive Art Gallery,
to your personal Magic Eye images.

The Monet shouts from that exuberance of king-cups
and reeds. Spy the moorhen in the foreground?

See this Van Gogh? Such brushstrokes suggest
the willow screamed through winter winds.

Of course this curve of the contoured cut
and the perfect O of a crumbling

rust-brick hump-backed bridge
must be mature Hepworths.

Peep over the hedge. Frick froze a mare
and her dancing foal on that green plinth.

The Hockney's sure to startle you:
a glint of trapped light in the water,

a diagonal of black lock beams
thrust against a flat blue sky.

Now – half close your eyes – don't you agree
this speckled afternoon is pure Seurat?

I think I can promise you another
surprising Turner at our supper mooring.

But we'll take our time. More masterpieces wait
round the curve and closing time is dusk.

Stealing Tixall Wide From The Staffs and Worcester Canal

One day I'll burst on Tixall Wide
curve on the sweep of an April dawn
hitch to a feather on the black swan's glide.
I'll dabble as giddy as a newborn
moorhen chick, full of scorn
for other birds and creep
under a mother's wings to sleep.

Or like a kingfisher I'll steal the Wide
for empire and rule its waters well.
To check my sphere below I'll slide
a rapier entry on a flashing swell
of blue electric. Though none may tell
my coming they'll learn to dread the shake
of teardrops in my soaring wake.

Like a coot that nests on a tyre
bobbing beside the towpath bank,
I'll wish that passers-by conspire
to leave me be; my head and flank
exposed but well ignored, my rank
forgotten. I'll rule alone
on a shining lily-lap throne

and be benevolent, the Wide
my chosen world. When I wish a boat
I'll charm the reed; let clouds decide
my toga, snow my winter coat.
I'll enchant the golden iris to moat
with fire these must-have broads,
to fence the realm with glowing swords.

Planning The Route

You said Woodseaves Cutting? Lucky you!
Though I'd tease if I say I knew it well.
I'd tell a lie.
I travelled through it only once
yet I know it in the way I fear old loves.

Past Holling's Bridge on the narrowed canal
grows a green cathedral
of outrageous leaves
and way-out shoots in a silent gloom
you could slice with a machete.

Stars confetti the water yet
the flow of day and night admits
no differences; light shimmers
under the surface in a quicksilver glow
like a ghostly net for unwary travellers.

Don't try to know more of Woodseaves' charm.
Avoid the lilting thought that you might linger.
Hold the tiller tight against harm and aim
arrow-straight for the high bridge
and no backward glance. Chances

are your days will pass in innocence.
As for me I burn in a rainbow
for ever landlocked
playing the elusive cinema
of Woodseaves' exotic leaves.

Mind how you go!

A Tillerman Addresses His Wife On The Craft
Of Narrowboating and Poetry

My dear, she's seventy feet
long and built like a Boeing
so like rhythm and rhyme
needs a master's hand.

So I'd best be in charge
of the mystique of steering
for she pivots as she answers
like a laid-back sonnet.

It's technical know-how
which is why I have a notebook
like a cleat to hang a line on
and a ring-bound thesaurus

to guide me on the side.
Now we're coming to a lock,
and you know it's child's play
to twiddle the paddle spindle.

Wear gloves with focussed seams;
grasp the windlass as firmly
as I on a wayward adjective.
You shove the lock beams

while I master verbs;
capture a tricky image,
the heady aroma of metaphor,
the slant of a theme.

I'll allow long vowels to echo
like globules in Shrewley Tunnel.

You know, steering a craft
takes testosterone

and clearly it's best
if I have the business in hand.
When I'm in the lock, drop
a half hitch over a bollard.

I'll figure a mooring for a poem
I hear powering along to a full stop.

Peg On *Argy Bargy* Tells It How It Is

In the prow most nights I try to wrap
the sky around me, and listen
to bankside reed blades rustle
and owl calls tingling the hair on my nape.

Since I turned my feet from city haste
and bought into the novelty of stars,
I've come alive in the ease of being
a snail cruising a silver thread.

There's something about the whispers
of wilderness that blows my mind. It's nature
rhyming to what's out there. When all
the navigation sings I want

to join the chorus rising to the stars.
If I fling out my arms I can fasten
on a curve of the universe,
swing on the rhythms of its psalms.

A morning swan comes out of the mist
glides in on a silver morning,
commands immediate attention
before I sort water, fresh bread, wine

and heed the wind and weather.
A kind blackbird sings away the haze
as far as the next lock, and I cruise
adventuring round welcomed bends

until dusk whispers *get the mooring pins,*
whistles me out again and the moon
beckoning over the prow charms me
and I rise to worship by learning to listen.

Narrowboat Log, Adderley Mooring

Dawn's well up, but I'm still watching
sunbeams steam dewdrops off the tiller
while a blackbird chirps in the nearby spruce.

There goes my swallow kissing the canal
as she breakfasts on splashes. I'll swear a smell
of autumn's off the grass today.

Shall I move on or shall I stay?
A fishing rod would feign a proper purpose
and then these quicksilver swallows

would stitch a stretch of languid days.
I'd listen out for creep of brambles;
moor till blackberries ooze out grubs,

be on watch in a cool light
for the spill of bats from Audlem's tower
to signal the shutdown of my night

and its blunt end. But that's years away.
Freedom's my preferred illusion
living for moments like this. Guess I'll stay.

Christmas On The Lancaster Canal

Creatures of course; rabbits watching
a robin perched on the tiller. Not much
of a show but a presence, like a nip in the air
or frost in a blue sky and a glad rise
of smoke from a wood-burning stove.

Presents of course; a lump of fat
on the hawthorn, peanuts on the towpath
paper cracking off books and boxes
of ginger. The smell of sage and onion
and a crunch of boots before a feast.

Stillness of course; the crack of ice
somewhere else, the little sounds
a landscape utters to listeners
caring for calm. Inside, the chink
of glasses and the smile in your eyes.

Opening The Back Door

This frosty dawn smells of
washing stiffened overnight
in the yard. At once
nothing matters for it arrives
with a remembrance
of somewhere else.

A blackbird cocks his head.
He watches me disappear
onto a towpath
by a hawthorn hedge
where mist whitens the water
and a small wind puffs away night.

One coral dawn like this
I saw a water vole tow
a curtain of lacewing ripples
across the canal.
In my mind I'll swim
after his tracery.

There'll be dew beading the grass
winking diamonds back to fading stars.
A day of flame will stretch out
to the horizon
and take me with it.
This rosy sky is everything.

In Praise Of Water

I'll roll up a meadow, hang it low
enough to admire its fringe of hawthorn,
its snowy arms linked with sloe.

Its cheerful promise will adorn
sullen days and wings waft
soft echoes of busy afternoons,

while under its breath, in limestone shafts,
fingering ways through secret channels
water works its wild blue arts.

Water at the craft of it, gouging tunnels,
grinding away. Sink holes
open in meadows, flumes funnel

down hillsides, widen a mole's
hard labour; rise into becks,
springs, wells, make a vole

retreat to a bank where a heron neck
bends. Here are caves unexplored,
drops unnamed, riverlets wreaking

sweet havoc on slopes scored
and scoured, gravel-scratched willow trees
by tributaries and all the poured
blessing of water leaping to the sea.

Breathing Elterwater

When I see you, I'll tell you
about daydreaming hours supine
under willows laying loose overshadows

watching reflections float
under swathes of trees pulling July down
from the clutches of flies on the shingle.

I'm a lazy escapee under birches
flavouring the evening with spirals of smoke;
I welcome silence delivered on the breeze

falling from Lingmoor Fell to Chapel Stile.
Sweeps of water powerfully pull me
to cool afternoons on a tranquil shore.

Reverie takes a long view –
off fell-top or lake shingle –
the lure of breathing an unframed scene.

Stars shrink me to a leaf,
I'm given a glimpse of a world in balance.
Clocks disappear, clouds lose relevance.

Grounded here this place feels
more like home than home ever did.
If I leave, I will tell you about it.

Catrigg Force

Like an elver I wriggle through the old gate stop-gap
   gurgle through shallows then headlong drop
      to roar my fury, to make sweet havoc.

I thunder cascades out of the gorge
   boil them up the lichened rock
      spray the Ribble deep below.

Droves of bikers and hikers
   and ill-shod day trippers
      watch me hammer out clefts and clints.

Perch on this shadow – I'll whisper that
   Turner stole light from my muted greens –
      feel the welcome chill on my breath.

Go if you must to Stainforth's teashop
   to snowdrops and winter aconites
      where I whisper foam onto the stepping stones.

Why aren't I left to my own devices?
   Don't quarrel with a river. Fools –
      you've blundered into my wilderness.

Swallowing The Kent

What did they feel, looking at the dull
foreignness of seemingly solid sand –
about the promise of welcome at Outcast
about a colony of healing at Lepersgarth,
about kindly monks at Conishead Priory –
what could they know of the treachery of sand?

They'd know of something rather like that
glimpsed in many a stranger's eyes:
the shifty fear, the turning aside –
they'd know about that kind of dread.
As they waited on Heysham shore
like boulders dumped by melting ice,

staring seawards to the spit of Cartmel,
hope might have risen under their rags,
for the King's Guide's to lead them.
He knows the trembling treachery of shifting
sands. A safe way to Far Ness
he's marked already with new-cut birch.

As they pray for the blessing of the sea's absence
they must hope he's been paid enough to keep faith,
while far out waves swell to a surge
faster than horses can splash through shallows;
the rioting horizon will lash a rebellion
propel the waves into funnels of the Bay;

roll over plumes of sandy banks
and swallow the Leven, the Kent and the Crake.
Did *they* know all this by the pale sands?
Yet some must have travelled well enough
to the block of stone hollowed for a scoop
of vinegar that cleanses a groat or a farthing.
Outcasts. At Lepers' Garth.

Sea Change

River Crake crawls from Coniston reeds,
  licks his hunger at the feet of yellow flag,
    bellies out to Allen Tarn.
      Pauses.

Sprawls in the silver midday heat;
  skin flattens in the millpond hush;
    sway of weed presses out
      slow breath.

Damselflies pinned in length like
  sapphires enamel his shimmering face,
    stitch reeds to fringe his body.
      Skin ripples.

Eels throb thin pectorals
  thrust power along his flanks,
    ease him over jostling pebbles.
      Force entry.

Cows ignored, he squeezes under
  bridges, slithers into Morecambe Bay,
    swells to a sly serpent lurking.
      Quicksand.

Sean's Undertaking

Most days in Armagh as he posted in a corpse
and smoothed out the coffin silks
or coaxed grey cheeks to bloom
his absent mind brushed oil on canvas
in his studio's cold white room.

Then, he said to me, one day
he'd be stripped in a box like this
with no waymarks set up anywhere
from life's rough track of travel
showing what way he'd paid the fare.

So he upped and off to sun and sand
where unclocked time is kind,
set an old easel down
to open the doorway to his dreams.
As for a critic, he'd be his own,

honouring the stirring in his blood.
He gave it recognition. He said
it was like unskinning onions
and last finding, a blast of sunlight.
Except that waking up, some dawns,

spitting blood from tender gums
or wrinkling his nose at hissing urine,
he said he sometime wondered if
he'd maybe left it a wee bit late.
'Still, better late than if only,' he sniffed.

'If only's a terrible thing sure
to be drumming down your days.
I'm set free here, here I'm out of my cage
keeping at bay a cotton shroud.'
He waved his brush as my ferry engaged.

The beach is away now but not Sean.
On this wall he's still works
under a red sky, on ochre sand;
honours the itch behind his eyes;
waves his brush towards me in his hand.

Bit o' Crack On The Fell

after Jiacopo di Cione, The Nativity

Lads were in a sweat of a hurry
but argued about leaving t'sheep.
Seth said it were too much of a worry
if all went. Wolves 'ud make us weep
over losses; best if someone stayed.
So dogs and Seth were left behind.
That were a mistake. It laid
us open to nagging; what kind

of chaps kings were, how dressed –
drove us daft wi' his shouts
for't tale again; how he pressed
and hinted at what we'd left out.
Said as he'd done his good turn
where were gold to grease his toil –
where his sweet sticks to burn –
where his share of the spoil?

We told him again about t'stall;
stinking lamps for light,
dusty hay, and the cattle all
blowing warmth at the mite;
them looking on as if mazed
would speak if they'd tongue,
as if they knew more than could say
at the wonder he might become.

We rounded on him – Seth!
We have been blest wi' a glimpse
o' glory and that's a wealth
enough for us – so whist!
Settle now and know
that yesterday when you stayed
out o't glittering show
you'd a big part to play.

Dost think we'd steal from a ewe
and her helpless wide-eyed lamb?
We'd sooner hunger and keep true
to the signs the angel sang,
fasten faith in a Lordchild's birth
than fail it for pieces of gold
wi' God riding down that light
to our bit of earth! Nay, Seth, be told.

Jan van Eyck Talks About That Portrait

If you ask me, she's proved herself –
his dad and mam desired to pass
the family name, the family nose,
so she's done all right, acceptable,
and they've given her ells of green velour
to bundle up the coming fondle.

I wondered what she was thinking about
but who asked her? Really asked
if she fancied that long nose, pale faced,
bony arse? She's married him,
done as she's told and that's that.

The bed's in the painting there, of course.
Significant that, rich silks and bolsters,
and the ruby drapes set off the green.
Ground floor, and open to the yard –
a bit downmarket I'd say, really
not what I'm used to nowadays
but the fetched-in mirror and candelabra
give sparkle to the whey-faced pair.

Very boring, no small talk
which I quite like when I'm working –
otherwise I whistle through my teeth,
if you know what I mean, tunelessly,
none of that street razzmatazz
crumhorns and tambour stuff,
no, I find a steady sibilance
keeps my hands moving nicely.

The greens I'm proud of, I could hint
the recipes, but not the quantities–
there's white in oil, yellow ochre
and lapis with a touch of burnt umber.
Last a few good years these hues,
outlive me and that's for sure.

I'll put in my famous touch of red –
say, a pomegranate in the window light –
not in the central line – no, no –
I'll shove their giving hands in there,
generosity preserved in paint.

Truth is, they're stingy. Not a bite
all the day. Had to ask for ale.
Came in the smallest firkin,
never a whiff of gravy crust.
'You'll have your own cheese.' The cheek!
Well, I've been better served in far
scurvier places than this grand house –
mean as the meat on a rabbit's foot.

I'll get my own back – make him thinner
and sneak my easel into the mirror.
Folks'll puzzle over that for months.
Symbolic, they'll call it, latching on
to their own preoccupations, so
my mirrored canvas will be time curving
into harmonious married days;
the bed will be the loving tie
and settlement of quietude;

the pomegranate a fecund globe
to signify progenic joys.

Even the pattens, placed as if
to leave the room, will turn to Time's
steady stride out of my painting
though what you make of that red cover
thrown over the spare coffin in the corner
I'm laughing to know, do whisper it to me.

Rat In The Frame

Mariana by Millais, 1850, Tate

So *he*'s not there, not human at least
if he ever was truly in the frame.
Each day she sits on her red suede seat

and endlessly eyes the garden gate.
The rat (whose apt name could be Angelo)
knows her routine. After a while

she'll stretch, languid in a spine-easing pose
he'll turn his whiskers as if to hide
and she'll freeze in her true-blue livery

as if an angelus had rung.
She'll watch the green leaves darken, blow in
decay to gold, come back again,

and only the oil-lamp's silver chain
will waft her love with its constant flame.
Her gown is glorious, crushed lapis lazuli,

whose velvet folds glowed
as they streamed from Millais' brush.
One day her prince will be repealed

but what virgin wants a heartless groom
who clearly has her measure?

Kurt Schwitters In Hanover, 1920

Herr Schwitters, how do you work?

I take what's to hand, work by addition –
without form – down with tradition!
A dialogue of self and materials; an incantation
that allows mistakes, won't sink a nation
nor summon the four horsemen to my door!

I demand from myself much more freedom to play
with all principalities of paint, of texture,
the enormity of making change happen
while observers experience totality serves
to excite me. This is Merz!

Merz hurls change,
works on the doer, says,
'Look at the beauty of life!
I am praise for gaiety, wit and fire.
Look afresh – see how I change the viewer!'

Herr Schwitters, what is Merz?

Merz art is self-contained,
refers to nothing external,
never defers to real life.
True art is abstract,
embraces a tube of paint, a song,

an impact of words, of lines.
It is a prayer about victory,
of peace won in the glare
of the world where all fragments.
Yet fragments grow new things

not in old ways but a new art that is Merz!
I reject the past – I look afresh
on wires or strings, paper or sticks,
being open to form; to steal
their possibilities is my norm!

Herr Schwitters, how does one make Merz?

Wire up lines that clamber ropes
of metal mesh, let them fight
amongst themselves then kiss
in tenderness. Points burst like stars,
roar through a storm, twist prehensile wires.

Throw white air softly through bright lights;
take wheels and axles, hurl them up.
let them sing; take a dentist's drill,
a scraper, broken cup, a tram ticket,
balloons – and change them!

All things to hand fuse into the work.
People can take part, can enter,
can walk on stage, beat a drum,
shout the text – become
the experience I call Merz!

Olga In The Red Dress

after Picasso, Portrait of Olga in an Armchair

The dancer in red
will rise from her chair
point elbows aside
put right foot in front.

Prrrr from guitarists
will throb out the call
for her steps to advance
and take up the pose.

Belly and buttocks flat,
shoulders held low
she points up her breasts
like the horns of a bull.

Clap clap stamp!
toe heel stab!
toe stab
heel stab
st-amp!

Now her dance
is zapat-
ea-do;
she flaunts
and flings

up her head
with her hips
on fire
and ratt-
ling claps

of her palms
to the side
again
again
again!

During arr-
ogant turns,
imper-
ious glan-
ces pierce.

Clap clap stamp
as the sol-
ea winds
to wild
fandango!

OLE!

FLAMENCO!

Portrait Of Her As A Sunflower

after Mary Fedden, R.A. *Sunflower*

This sunflower's in a black vase
for black's a mirror face of lust, he says.
The chopped-up lime is how he feels
whenever passion strikes.

And that's his heart in every slash
of fuchsia pink and burning red –
as if paint could patch the torment
of wanting only her.

Laughter bouncing off the tray
is jaunty, fond, exuberant,
but her smile's a lemon slice, he says.
His point of no return.

He says he tried to write a cheerful verse
that told the truth of wanting her
in images that lied about
the heave of his desire.

He says he tried to squeeze his love in song:
to conjure out of three chord tricks
the lure of coaxing her until
the cadences collapsed.

He says he tried to paint her loving face
caress her cheek with careful strokes
let a brush explore the flesh
he could not, dare not touch.

But in the end he cut her up
and furious, like a sabre slash
he wrecked her sunshine cheeks with strips
of burnt sienna slats.

I'm Taking Tea On The Terrace
after Sue Macartney-Snape

with Kitty, Clarissa and Kate
I'm tête-à-tête below the topiary
in a tinkle of china;
the delicate calm of an English afternoon
poured from a Georgian teapot.

In slender chiffons
under straw hats,
casting disdainful glances at noises off
they are polite to a visitor
who goes hatless in the heat.

They hold the languid pose of old money.
It's green diets keep their figures trim,
it's green moods stipple their yellow age
among box hedge regimented
like Grandar's infantry at Omdurman.

While the strawberry tart's for show,
a thin slice from the chocolate cake
poses on Royal Doulton.
Earl Grey scents the terrace. Beyond,
concrete threatens their brittle diction.

This I may tell in an afternoon's
tête-à-tête on their estate
with Kitty, Clarissa and Kate.

Still–Life With Strawberries

When a restful day threatens of sweat under shade
on the patio table there'll be strawberries for tea
and the fevers of bees in the fragrance of jasmine
rise in my head and drum out smiles
of how good it is to dine in the sun.

If strawberries today, why not every day?
And why not take our treats on an ex-pat beach?
I'd leave off pouring from this home-thrown pot
and serve white porcelain's pale Darjeeling
while we linger by a turquoise pool.

How good could be our companionable years
until wrinkles coffin our pensioned bones,
yet once we're committed to living out there
would the loom of each day weave a worry
of how we speed our moments in the sun?

A working hand's such a blessing, such a boon.
To capture the phoenix in the mind as she rises,
shape into a form that did not exist at dawn,
so satisfies. Damping down a vision
may kill more than I can guess.

If I beckon on idleness, how shall I relish
a daybreak rising onto arid reality?
I see there's more than strawberries on the table.

With Mrs Tennyson In The Morning Room At Farringford

And Life with the Great Poet?

I feel so privileged, being Alfred's helpmeet
copying his works, for his hand is clarity itself.
All correspondence I attempt to answer in his style
and ink the pens for signatures during tea.

Interests?

Oh, yes, indeed, of course I have.
His poems I set to music on the pianoforte
and compose the hymns for family celebrations.
Between ourselves, my dear, I confess
to writing fiction of an autobiographical derivation,
but pray don't make a note of that,
for he does not know, but it is a comfort
that I might show it to the grandchildren.

Encouraged?

I always have, yes, indeed.
Being late to marry at thirty-six,
I had a very full life before and during
our long engagement, when dear Alfred
and I together made a name for him.

Family Life?

He's built a sphere of love around us
in the houses I run, both here and Aldworth.
So much to thank God and dear Alfred for,
so much, so much, and bless him,
he allows me to place upon his desk

handwritten notes (in what he charmingly
calls 'my poetic prose') on subjects
he might care to work up into poems.

Ah, yes – your Interests?

Though not so much of late have I attended
to his needs, being easily fatigued
with a weary dragging pain that chains
me to this sofa, and dear Alfred
is so patient with what he terms
'a womanly trouble'. He is my rock,
my fortress and my strength.
What would I do without him?

A Literary Reviewer To A Fellow Poet

As far as I can see, women writing
poetry are like Morris men larking
with sticks and bells – irrelevants to be ignored.
And a pale whisper if unfortunately
they're invited to read – Heaven forfend!
Here's a book of poems by a woman writer –
I'm supposed to review it differently?
That's what Tom said. Well, not quite.
Seems they want to be looked at in a special
kind of light. The glare of compassion?
Look here. At least a forename, not initials.
Assume a crisis over the Fairy liquid,
a storm-tossed heart, a parent's wilt,
bodily functions &/or fluids, a cat –
and they expect a good review of all that?

You'd think they'd learn on the job like us,
networking drinks in late night bars.
Look here – on this pile I've Grecian myths
lyrically rendered by a particular chum;
a play in verse, a clever translation
(my old Oxford tutor, I was another
of his protégées); a first collection
by a promising Glaswegian – sure of a Gregory.
More *Selecteds* from our favourite editors –
you know the usual sort of global view
they deliver – truly amazing insights
focus, point up, illuminate; power
readers' appreciation, sales figures and tower
over the poetry world where I the prominent figure
asks – 'Why can't women write with our ambitious vigour?'

Eavesdropping On Narrative

If I wait on her daily, about this time
she'll unlatch the door to my mind.
It's better for me if I get there first.

I close my eyes to imagine a situation,
breathe deeply, no more hesitation.
I'm wading in a familiar pool.

I follow the flow, let the clouds clear,
hoping my main character, that's Daniel,
is near enough to smell. A great detail

to write, seeming a memory
of what's yet to come. The fun
lies in unravelling struggled years

of childhood, loving deeds, fears
of secrets known, any guilt he owns.
There may be a sense of my soul

showing through in his growing: hints
of similar faults and fusses as I slant
a mirror at his terrors. But I won't hold

back, I'll shove at any wall.
His smile widens; I'll see him walk
across the page, hear him talk

when he thinks he's alone. The muse
rewards me daily. Opening the door is all.

Tall Grass Boasts Of The Tiger

I wait his pleasure for he is all majesty –
in silence or in fury – he's here! Here! He's now!

How his bones press me! Proudly I cherish his claws!
I taste the musk of his parts while his tail caresses.

I flame in his fur when he stretches his terrible limbs.
The cunning of his sinews I adore and my roots reverberate

in his growl. He blinks when I kneel to the pounce of his paws.
I glorify the crunch of kills for blood he gifts

to me and weight of his droppings warms the snow.
A rumour of fear through the forest shouts his scent

and hooves panic their echoes after I'm still.
I crouch until a veil of shadow covers

as he shivers light into splints of bronze shade.
All warmth in the forest he empties with his cold eyes

as he rises; this is the way of it always
tall grass and tiger together and I grow

in the blood and bone of him, and to him alone
I bow, for only I may hug the tiger.

Apple Tree

While the house creaks under its heat
the apples flame against the hedge.
Blackbirds note the clusters

and make experimental stabs.
The sun presses the apples,
transfers red flush to their skins

and warms the ripest for the wasps.
Twin fruits are cuckoos in the nest:
tight-yoked under the sprigs

one swells and dooms the other.
Clearing the onions, we hear
the soft thud of a heartbeat.

'More for the wasps,' we say.
They mob the bruises, tunnel in,
tumble out. Tipsy on liquor

they lie on their backs and kick
in a kind of prayer.
We leave them an apple or two.

Ulverston

a tumble of pebbles
scooped up from the shore

flung beyond marshland
out of the Bay

running waves
of cobbles and yards

alleys tunnelling
off thoroughfares

in stone gray facades
neighbourly grown.

January In Ulverston

Day sulks, sits about snivelling
eyes raining with cold, depressed.

Night arrives uninvited at teatime;
feet under the table, sits out the coals.

Misses the last bus so kips on the slates,
spreads a white sheet over the chimmucks.

It's a toe-cold time in attic bedsits.
Icy filigree blooms on the glass.

Day heaves out of a pewter sky,
looks to bring a touch of colour to the streets.

Shines a wakeup for starlings who clatter
off like an all-expenses committee.

Everything's an effort, roll on spring,
says snivelling day to a yellow crocus.

It's hinder, spite, and sly begrudgement,
January is. Night grins behind the wheelies.

Pokes an exploratory icicle. *Get you later,*
it whispers. *I'd leave now if I were you.*

Ambushing Spring At Swarthmoor Hall

'Up periscope!' orders a daffodil. 'It's half-past
January! Go and see what's happening up there.'

Rank and file snowdrops snap to attention,
thrust pale spears through the turf to test the frost.

Blasted by sleet they report in some disorder.
'Trench!' shout the dozing bluebells. 'Not yet!'

Trapdoors of frost spring down on quivering shoots.
Narcissi duck their heads in case of sabotage.

Violets shrink in relief, glad of a longer siege
but purple crocuses reckon up tactics,

decide to go over the top regardless of a predicted
wind-chill factor on late-night news.

Lined up in battle formation, they flaunt their colours,
prepare to take the field through frost, flood, snow.

Onions and Other Intentions

when frost tracks inside the clods
explodes them to bullets
it's time to wait

when the glow of Christmas fades
to despair think about
some good new growth

when the sun on window slats
creeps on a strip each week
hold back alert

when greenness nourishes white-
hot shoots to excitement
begin to hope

when water from the black butt
drips warm into buckets
it's time to act

At The Foundling Hospital

I   **Foundling 14928, 7th August, 1758**

Black ball, red ball, Heaven-sent white;
named as maybe, baptised perhaps.

A token pinned to each right-hand entry,
each for a child saved in love:
a scrap of gingham, calamanco, silk,
linsey-woolsey, flannel, serge.

'Letter in the blanket, sir.'

'Read it, ma'am.'

*'"He has had the breast and 'tis humbly hoped
'twill be continued as he will not
in all probability live without it."'*

'Thank you, ma'am, what fits the list?'

'Sleeves: 2.   Cap: with trim.
Bodice coat: white flannel.
Clout: a rag.   Stockings: 2,
blue yarn.   Shirt: Irish trimmed.'

'There, Foundling 14928's
entered, so give him to clean.'

Over the page black ink shines
on Foundling 12929's
inventory and the waiting pin.

'Cap, biggin, forehead cloth,
robe,long stay, frock, uppercoat, coat,

bodice, barrow, mantle, clout
sleeves, bib, neck-cloth, blanket,
waistcoat, stockings, shoes, shirt?'

'There's none o' them at all, sir,
only a girl in a workhouse shawl
and a scrap o' letter tucked in neat.'
"St Luke's Parish, Mary Dorking.
Child will be called for, pray take care."
No token, sir.'

      'Cut a corner to spare.
Then take it to clean and a spoon of gin.'

II   The Charity Draw

Patrons arrive with linkmen and lanterns
sweep past the queue to the drawing room.

Candlelight shines on the silks of the worthies,
a gathering seen to be doing good.

'Step forward, girl, this is the way of it.
Hold the child steady, put a hand in this bag.'

'Black ball, red ball, Heaven send white.
Pray let my baby be taken tonight.'

'Draw forth a ball onto this tray.
There's need to see the fairness of it.'

'Black ball, red ball, Heaven send white.
Pray let my baby be taken tonight.'

'Hurry up, witnesses wait,
your queue is long. Fetch one out.'

'Black ball, red ball, Heaven send white.
Pray let my baby be taken tonight.'

Crack on the tray falls a black ball.
Aghast is the mother – tears in her eyes;

turns away to the opened door,
stumbles out into the gloom.

Moonlight shines on fields open
down to the Thames running softly,

softly enough for a barge at anchor,
running softly for a chambermaid.

'Black ball, red ball, Heaven send white.
Pray let my baby be taken tonight.'

III   The Book Of Hope

A despairing mother, never reading
letters in her short life, knew the book
gave a future to a babe by her leaving.

Prosperity might come and a later look
for the child might make righteous her claim
to offer home to seamstress, joiner or cook.

Here's a ribbon and a Christening name;
the mother fled, afterlife glows off the page:
another babe saved for the survival game.

Fleshed on the bones of new name and age,
steps Thomas Brown, apprentice farrier
of fourteen years and strong, shoeing stage-

coach teams, meeting his mother Harriet
to fetch him home where she's making her mark.
What words can break the stone of Time's barrier?

This page is a promise; we're mother, baby, clerk
yoked by cotton, linen, wool; we're candlelight
before the boy fades into the dark.

At Tegg's Nose Quarry, Macclesfield

Look at this. I cleave it
and it rives in two
new as a bairn's bottom,
never had daylight
for millions of years.
A river of muddy sand
crushed by its weight
into this bonny beauty.

True grit's pink as bacon,
a rough buff pink,
crisp as crackling,
lovely to handle.
Shale's bloody useless --
that's up at top under sod.
Best grit's deep in bowels,
hard work to get.

You feel it, you work it
and you understand cold.
We drills a hole, hammers in
two metal feathers and a plug
till the stone rives off.
A crowbar helps, and then
a chisel splits it open.
We cut grooves, neaten edge.

Feel this slopstone.
Corners like the inside of your elbow,
very difficult. My work.
We made all manner of things.
Slopstones, paving flags
drain holes, mill stones

roof slates, grave stones
gate posts and kerb sets.

Yon dry stone wall
has a gritstone lintel
set above the sheep hole.
I sharpened knives
for me mam on yon grindstone.
Butters Powered Derrick
Crane shifted slabs
and Jaw Crusher riddled

roadstone out of waste.
Noise? I can't tell you.
Now sithee, behind this hut
see this stone, it's mine.
Carved it years afore.

'Here lies Jesseth Macabody, quarryman,
born 1934, died 20 . . .'
I told 'em I want to carve final figures.
They promised I can,
so I come up every day
just in case, just in case.

No Longer Solo

Jane loves the harmonies –
her own voice singing seconds
with her friend whose first soprano
line is chiming in her ear.

She's often run-down tired but
the conductor energises them.
She leaves with music singing
through her brain.

And as she rests her head
on the silent homely pillow
soprano lines crescendo
bars of melody in bed.

Her friends flock to the concerts
three or four times every year
when the Mayor of Drayton's chain
blazes in her shining eyes;

the clapping and the cheers
run round the church like fires
that warm her wintry streets
to home and drive her

looking forward to
fresh music in performance
with her friend the first soprano
at her side.

Uncle Arthur's Lilies Of The Valley

In the dawn of his life he crouches, adores
face to face their perfumed flesh,
wonders at their strange silence
in a sooty street ringing with handbells.

During hot afternoons of playing alone
he pokes black tar out of cobble seams
and with shreds of coated stalk swaggers
as if to work with a drooping Woodbine.

On the Home's armchair of an evening
his book of recollections falls
open on the waxy flesh
that sings of beauty beyond the dust.

Their nodding keeps him company;
perfect always, white bells of innocence
that never rang him into richer soils
nor kept their promise of a brighter light.

Always bonny, he whispers, being
faithful to the soft spring leaves,
the scented bells in his Mam's front garden
growing nowhere else he's ever been left.

Aunty Eva Under Pendle

Reedyford, Higherford, Roughlee and Watersmeet:
sunshiny paddlings and lifting of pebbles,
monkeys in cages and red hoopla stalls,
goes on the swing boats with my Aunty Eva
all to myself and no one to share.

Adored Aunty Eva ran out of the mill
to a glamorous job in a Midland hotel.
She's not often home, so today is a treat
and we're swinging up higher to kick away clouds
before asking a cottage to brew us some tea.

There's a twist of tea leaves in a bit of brown paper
and milk's in a bottle with a papered screw top.
We sit on their bench and scoff up our butties
while stewy smells waft from their open green door
then we walk the stream from Roughlee to home.

And each waft of Hovis out of a bakery,
conjures up the sunshiny day,
when Aunty Eva and I share a swingboat
and Heaven's a harvesty Hovis aroma
and sips of tea from a Bakelite cup.

Options Open

Black mill monster
clattering soot;
hot pungent cotton

through gaping doors;
cobbled ginnel
to primary school.

Stench of oil
tethers tacklers;
one's escaped

its black mouth.
Briefly beached
on a sunlit shore

he smokes a Woodbine
in the millyard dawn.
Hello, Dad.   'Hello, love.'

A weaver stands
in floral apron
at looms that count

her beads of sweat
by relentless clacks
that throb through

wooden soles
to varicose veins.
Quick fingers

twitch a knot,
mend the warp
before the shuttle flies

out at elbow
to punish
short-sightedness.

Ta-ra, Mam.
'Run along, love
or tha'll be late.'

Ta-ra Dad.
'Larn tha' lessons
or tha'll end up here.'

Ta-ra Mam.
Goodbye, millyard,
good riddance.

Envy

forced an entry. Dwells under my eaves.
Grows in my rafters like dry rot.

Grotesques snigger in every attic corner
ears cocked, eyes watchful and sly.

I can't endure this monotonous moan.
Unspoken words fester in the cellar

where stoppers burst from smelling salts
and vermin thrive in the ammonia air.

Shine your torch. It's overgrown wormwood
bitter, stinging, sour on my taste buds,

a red-raw sore that weeps at a glance.
Nothing good will come of it. Burn it.

The Terrible Mirror

It's true that if
you could put on a scale
the population of England
it would nicely balance
the weight of flies killed
by spiders every year.

All that going on!
Yet if I put my lost love
for you in one pan
and your regard in another
I know damn fine there'd be
no equilibrium.

Suppose we stood before
the jackal-headed god
who said my heart was fine
and truthful to behold,
what would he say of yours
that wreaks sweet havoc?

Were I Anubis
I should dash the scale
and let your blood cleanse
my terrible mirror
of memory. Red globules
I'd blow with my rage

to steal every puff of wind
from your lusty sails.
Long and bright would grow
the glow of your blood
to swell a river
whose name is vengeance.

You may stand and bleed
at these waters, hear
the pause and drop
of the scales under you
and I will rejoice at your terror
and be comforted.

To My Dear Valentine

*A found poem based on a Northern Arts circular to Writers
in the Cultural Industry*

I have researched the impact of your presence
and its attendant joys
and set them against the inner
needs of my cultural industry
and find that I am anxious
to stimulate sustainable employment,
and career development
within the over-arching framework
of your professional arms.

I would focus your attention therefore
on possible delivery mechanisms
for I am happy to research
the impact and your needs.

Though this strategy is demand-led
it is nevertheless a consultative process;
I feel we can incorporate all your desire
if you align it with mine.

Please signify
in an appropriate way
if you aspire to work
in the lower cultural sector
and want to experience my central philosophy
on the inception of the project in totality.

The deadline is fast approaching
and your cooperation in this enterprise is vital.

Shall I open my portfolio?

Break The Glass

The track's hidden as we enter the wood
where leaves are silent though a cloud grumbles
and rain tastes of mushrooms.

No need of words, the silence speaks to us;
oak and alder mutter green drops
to guide us companionably.

And here's delight, chestnut's tree-house
roped and sparred, rigged for sail
and I, Garbo in the wave-racked prow

will toss away a throne and with a lover
speed on an ocean of togetherness.
My scarf flies in the breeze

grass hisses under the prow
and when at last I turn to you
on our green-splashed deck

we'll mirror our delight in rain
break cold cocoons of separateness
and kissing kiss, holding tight

as one new self spreads wings in flight.

Guest Room

A white cotton handkerchief
under a stripped bed.
Nothing else, not a leaf

of a letter in a room shed
of laughing breath;
the waft of Chanel fled

out the door's the death
of you. Of us both.
There's nothing healthy

left in a room I'm loath
to leave though I can't remain.
Everything gone, nothing to gain.

A Late Love Poem

I didn't think I'd feel like this
when I bumped into you on the Penrith line

after twenty-four years
three months and seven days.

I didn't think it would feel like a guard
demanding the fare I'd already paid.

List Before Departure

I'll put it on the list: that in the yard
I saw in the dawn mist
sweet jasmine open its twists
of trumpets that the bees frisked

and beyond the door leading to the lane
pink foxglove urged its store
of nectar up to light, poured
out leaves for rough tongues to core

and Painted Ladies danced over windfalls
in tipsy innocence,
doing ballet on the chance
of an orchestra of ants.

Yes, head all lists with this: in the backyard
I smile in a dawn mist
as jasmine opens its twists
of trumpets for bees to kiss.

O.S. 775 930

No whisper, no rustle, no movement among
tussocks of stubble where a silent stream led
from Grisedale top down a bare brown fell.
'Strange, no wind, so quiet,' we said.
Then far away there shunted the noise
of a drumming on rails at Garsdale Head
fade out and in and a distant train
throbbed over the fell and nobody said
a word as we listened, but knew the sound
to be a comfort in the rough bed of the dale.

And none of us spoke as we walked the track
and saw a horse, or maybe a cow
(too far up the dale to be really sure)
or a sombre ghost in gray and brown
who once dwelt here beyond oath and law,
and we reached a barn and marvelled how
the Quaker fold had managed to farm
and who would choose this refuge now
with abandoned walls and muted birds
and soil that won't take the depth of a plough.

The quietness festers, hinders the leaving.
No need to go, for silence feels good
as it scoops us up like the arms of a lover.
Perhaps we might take root like the wood
of the slanted trees, bare branched now,
berries long gone? Maybe the stream would
entice us to linger? Its flow is the slender
braid of a fancy that perhaps we could
match the flame of passionate Friends.
A cold wind shivers a hint that we should
be gone. Grisedale's for the strong in spirit.

Invitation To A Meadow

Come to a meadow in sun or rain –
always glorious interest, startling,
that seriously entertains

study; ramble alongside bling-bling
jewels of bright yellow in May.
What's about landscape that makes us sing

its praises? We say 'Lovely! And way-
marked!' as if only that matters,
as if a stroll by a river passes a day

out the house. Landscapes replenish
the spirit, that poor unacknowledged
child of our time, who may astonish

with its own rich harvest if encouraged
by a quiet dressing of green meadow,
where a dialogue with unmasked self is language

stripped of any lie that casts a shadow
like a thing that should as well
have been left unsaid, whose sad echoes

resonate further than one can tell.
Here is unfiltered experience,
for a living dale casts its spell

and kindness to self swells in its influence.
Companioned by like-minded cherishers
of landscape, an eager audience

hears the Dee's nourishing overtones,
their crescendo and diminuendo, flow
through the beauty of a flowering meadow.

Giving Tongue

Melancholy thistle, stitchwort,
chickweed, ragged-robin,
forget me not, bistort –

a ploughman knew the old names,
knew when hooves would slow
the promise lurking in the sods he tamed,

while jackdaw and wintering snipe in a fallow
meadow picking for pignut roots
knew seeds by their fragrance under the snow.

Another language sprouted shoots –
a bloom of Latin on Yorkshire ground:
vulgare, officinalis, hirsutus

repens, sempervirens, and found
with *irritans, lanatus, palustris,*
would infiltrate his tongue's rich sound.

Lovely and Lush

                    lean the flowers of marsh
and mud: golden kingcup, red campion,
purple loosestrife and fresh

brooklime couched by a stream on
the slope whistled at by wagtails
and swifts. A rare place to dream on

a tranquil afternoon in this sun-raked dale,
where a bumble like a baby sumo
wrestles a blue crane's-bill

and I crouch in a quiet hay meadow,
listen for a honey bee and hover fly,
watch a trundling beetle and lie doggo

if I hear a circling skylark cry
over scoops of meadowsweet as high
as cow parsley perfuming the bee's home-run :
over the hedge, south of the sun.

Clock's Ticking, Farmer!

Rhianthus minor

I'm open-mouthed and purple-toothed,
hear my pepperpot seed-head prattle
in the breeze when I tittle-tattle

'Time to get up, get cracking on the hay
grown tall from seedlings quickened in May –
wheel out your machines on a July day!'

I push down suckers into grasses' roots
and steal their minerals as I raise my shoots
clear of trampling hooves or boots.

I fetch up iron, I fetch up zinc
I keep your winter beasts in the pink –
yellow rattle, yellow rattle, tink, tink, tink.

Gathering The Goodness

This field's hayed in late July.
We lets it lie and turns it over
next day we turns again to dry

and sets in rows. Led by clover
all the flowers have dropped their seeds
and now the baling machine recovers

rainblest leavings from fragrant weeds
and we bales into warm blocks of hay,
raw winter's precious feed

from untroubled exuberance of May.
Our beasts show off the power of dolly mixture
weeds to lay a nutritious buffet

by their sleek coats of healthy texture.
We'll have fewer bills from vets
during winter's coming fixture.

Until late autumn the meadow rests
while wind and weather determine its days,
then our stock comes in to graze again
on new grass grown with healing rain.

The Bundle On The Dresser

A Cumbrian farmer wants his son to follow him on the farm. Then foot and mouth disease arrives.

The Bundle On The Dresser

February, 2001

Here's Tom, up from the village
where his farm slopes above Frostrow
well out of harm's way of village lads
and second-home owners, the school, the pub
the post office cum grocers.

He's busy now with sheep,
gentling a lamb cupped in his hard hands;
stows it to its mam, and smiles in glad hope
of a good new stock of sturdy lambs
from his prize-winning Herdwick flock.

Dorrie, his wife on a much-needed
town-shop wage, says she feels
a village is centre stage to her vision
of well-managed hillsides dear to farming folk
that she holds clear in her mind.

'I've got a thousand pities
for millions forced to live in stuffy cities
where friendly nods attract
sideways looks and like-minded folks
can only meet in books

or clubs or Internet chatroom browsing.
They mun be lonely folk,' she says,
delousing the sheep dog Jessie,
then scrubbing her hands she's off and ready
to midwife newborn lambs

fettle the tractor, whip up W.I. cakes,
do the farm accounts,
and daily tries to make the oil
of their hard-working lives easier flow –
as long as she's on hand to make it go.

March - Army Butchers To Work In Cumbria

A chilling wind blasts from the east.
Tom recalls his father's woes
flings wet mats down at his gate
paints warning boards that say KEEP OUT.

One dawn the yard shades over in shreds
of sediment and blackened straw.
'That's the writing on the bloody wall,
that's too near for comfort, Dorrie.

'Look at yon hedge I cut backend
slashed to slivers of sapwood. I know
shoots'll grow tidy up to the light
though it's years afore we see results.

'If them blundering officials has their way
they'll hedge Cumbria with fire and vets
and we'll see results of that too soon
and mun live with whatever shoots grow out of it.'

April 27th, 2001.   Crake Valley, Cumbria

Winds of change raged down the fell,
ravaged lambs, kids and calves;
blasted Lowick's and Low Nibthwaite's
fields and savaged Blawith's.

Singed the fleeces, raddle-marked
like crimson targets for a gun;
blew in the nostrils of the dead
swelling in the sun.

Roared over cordoned roads,
slapped on stickers of cancelled shows;
swept out spiders from cavernous beams ,
silenced the stalls and rows

of bright machines in echoing sheds;
hustled tails from sacks of feed;
rustled rosettes nailed to the walls:
'First Prize – Best of Breed.'

Ravens poke at the tall grown fields
in uniform like a constabulary team
conducting a blade to blade
search of the yellow-taped scene.

Bone and muscle of Angus beef
is scorched like the track in a Swaledale's brain;
blown are the sifted genes of each kind,
gone, gone with the April rain.

***

Cushions of cream
blossom the sloe bush
conceal black thorns
from Tom at his gate.

Dewdrops bead the sheep's wool.
She shifts, she's uncomfortable.
There's a wall-eye glint in her eye.
Her well-sorted destiny

is going to plan.
Black feet emerge.
She turns her head, licks
off the lamb, liberates it

to the smell of freedom.
Its fleece begins to dry.
She notices no one,
for she's not finished -

here's a second set of hoofs.
Her eyes focus; Tom nods.
As she grunts in satisfaction
a van creeps through the mist.

A white-coat flicks his pen.
With a mark like a slash from a thorn
her history's rewritten.
Tom at the gate clutches his head.

Postal Deliveries Resume

The report shakes in his hand.
The kitchen table vanishes
his world spills open.

The thing he fears
squats on the page.
'Necessary steps.'

The paper drifts from his hand
his fingers cradle his eyes
while all his days that led

him to this text
shatter into dust.
He is naked as a new-hatched.

His howl explodes
in particles of torment.
He stares at his hands, his feet;

even his boots seem not his own.
Nothing is, not even his breathing
nor any reply to the text.

***

When they phone their college son
Dorrie weeps. 'Such black days, Peter!
The stink of the trampled dead and terrified
taints the air we're sucking in!

'And Dad whistling down our futures
pitching our livelihood at the guns
and me as helpless as a washer woman
might wring her hands by a dry river bed
while raging waters dammed inside me!'

'I'm up at dawn with the dogs,' says Tom.
'A wagon team first, then slaughtermen and vets.
Two mates with their dogs and me on the quad,
setting out on two thousand feet of snow and fog,
mirr thick as a dollop of bread sauce
and sheep in thousands, not one to be missed.
They falls out of cloud like sand grains
through an hour-glass. That's our life draining away,
I think. I'm crushed by the sight of them.

'We circle them in fog and sort them below to hurdles,
dogs like ribbons tying sheep to the pens,
and vets, slaughtermen, waggoners, waiting,
waiting, fagging it, swearing it, waiting.

'Stink of acid, the squash of fleeces,
sweat scorching my nostrils like needles of fire,
the shite, the urine, the blood – oh!
the blood everywhere, Peter!

- 79 -

A stench to cut with a knife and never get rid!
My flesh gone numb with the slaughter
and the rotten stink of the bolt-guns.

'Day never ending,
till the setting sun flames the fell
like the pyres my stock burns on –
like it gives permission for anger to melt
into tears and they fall in the stinking yard
and the fuck fuck fuck of the killing men stop.

'When wagons drive off I shuts the gate
but were only out of habit.
Oh lad, how the stillness infects!
Silence, everywhere, silent.'

May, 2001

He stumbles out of the house,
through the open barn doors.
'What more could I have done?'
he shouts to the dust in the emptied barn.

'It were like a cloud – so long we'd lived with it –
no sleep – under prison sentence!'
Frantic to keep control of his world
he fingers sacks and bundles of twine.

***

'Echo, I mun talk it out though your whispers'll mock me.   *me*

I know your gross replies will satisfy no one
like me who's frantic to tek it in,   *in*

- 80 -

who may cry over his naked fields
and never know another soft night's sleep.   *sleep*

Rumour rubbed out my forecast of shorn fleece
and there's nowt that weighs in on my side   *side*

there's no light shining on this mischief.   *chief*

It's clear a hand's hard work may give none
a secure clutch on a livelihood,   *hood*

mun only postpone the minute when we mum count
how much longer the bones of our days
can tend these fells.   *fells*

Who knows when this bitter war in Cumbria'll be won? *won*

There's no one to say when ways be clear!   *clear!*

No one! No one.   *No one*

June, 2001

When Dorrie's kept out of his Five-Mile Zone
he stumbles through tears to the empty kitchen
throws bits and twists of twine on the dresser
and stares red-eyed at deserted fells
while April soot from Orton taints
the windowsills and yard.

He slumps in his old low rocking chair
and hears his father, mother, gran
speak of years living with the land
while he's blown like the ash of his slaughtered stock
in unpaid bills and leaking slates.

The men who cleared and sheared and scythed
and women who span, preserved and milked
and turned their toil to babes and bread
call him from the raw fell-side.
'Endure! You can endure! Survive!'

'Leave me be! I'll not be pressed!
You're only ghosts – get back beyond!
I'll not heed your cries! Where's the brass
that's needed now? Where's your legacy?'

He paces across the kitchen flags
the worn rugs, through lonely rooms.

'I can foretell wind and rain
shear a fleece quickest hereabouts
cure the fluke, the rot, the ticks,
cut the hay and train a dog.
What use are them beyond yon track
interfering buggers feel free to come down?'

There's no touch upon his hand or mind
that tells him grief like his is shared
is understood. He's failed his son
made penniless the boy's ambition.

He sits and rocks as silence grows;
lays his anger on the cold hearth
of his family name, and hears again

'Endure! You can endure!'

It floats out to the purple hills
where his student son worries on
a letter he might or might not post.

Dear Dad,

        For long I've thought on what to say
and it isn't easy; I know you want me to succeed
and follow you on, but some days I can't see the way
through, like a track to a field's overgrown with weed
and you can't see a gate, and if you could, you know you'd find
it barred and high to climb, and you'd twist all round.
Do you understand? Can you touch my mind?
I'm saying I can't stay on here, Dad, I can't. The ground's
unworkable; my back's not skinned with your kind of hide.
The hills that bind and the sheep that shaped your hands
can't toughen mine, though God knows I've tried
to please you, but I glimpse in me a land
where beasts and binder twine can't work the themes
that tug me now through all my waking dreams.
              Oh Dad, your way of life can't be my future!
                    Your loving son Peter

August 29th, 2001

Tom rummages in his toolbox
to give himself a job to do
a reason to stay on here, now
holding steady, holding trim.

The stubborn gate has sunk into the grass.
He prises rusted hinges off
while Jessie cocks her head and waits.

The gate rests. He'll oil the hinges
when the claw hammer and old chisel
sit back snugly by the screwdriver;
everything in order; holding on.

***

He slumps in the kitchen rocking chair.
broods on another gate closing fast
that he's powerless to halt with any
wedge of thought he can summon.

He's of a mind that skids away
desperate to settle somewhere else,
through another gate to a way unknown.

A signpost perhaps could do the trick?
He'll have to make one for himself,
give a name he'll recognise, acceptance
being part of what the name must do.

He'll make it out of hours alone
build in the white noise of night,
a sign to tell him where he's going.
Forward the finger points or back –
resist or retire, restock or regret.

If only it was a bridge – that would be
a fine thing – stone by stone
a bridge builds a new road
but a signpost must be conned in an instant
or not at all, and that's the grit
in his eye that blinds. If only,
if only he knew what to do for the best.

***

He lurches towards the twine on the dresser
senses the sanctuary of a merciful grip
whose fingers point to a safer haven
and Self dictates that he must follow.

Black despair darkens his mind;
Self centers on the right solution.
Dorrie and Peter die in his heart.

Shadows hasten from dark corners
'You can endure – survive, survive,'
the creeping voices murmur again,
'Survive!'

Whispers rise to insistent shrieks –
his step halts on the cold flagged floor –
his outstretched hand stops on the twine.

'SURVIVE'

Jessie stamps her paw on his boot
grounds his mind to a need elsewhere.
He fumbles with her biscuit box,
scatters crumbs, her tail wafts his legs.

'You can endure!'

Dorrie breathes as if she's close
Peter's face hovers before him
the darkened room of shadows lightens.

The voices back him into the doorway.
He turns and stumbles into the yard
breathes in the bright blue air.

Sunshine beckons from life-affirming
hill and hedge and high-grown field.

'Survive!'
He's off at a run over the grid
to warmer voices down in the village.
Flowing behind him Jessie follows
scenting the wind of a new direction.

The voice fades, the rocking chair slows
the sneck clamps down on the kitchen door.

Dust begins its work of settling
on a bundle of twine on a kitchen dresser
in a slate-cold farm on Frostrow Fell.

Indigo Dreams Publishing
132, Hinckley Road
Stoney Stanton
Leicestershire
LE9 4LN
www.indigodreams.co.uk